WHY DO PLATYPUSES LAY EGGS?

AND OTHER CURIOUS MAMMAL ADAPTATIONS

BY PATRICIA FLETCHER

Gareth Stevens
PUBLISHING

Please visit our website, www.garethstevens.com. For a free color catalog of all our high-quality books, call toll free 1-800-542-2595 or fax 1-877-542-2596.

Cataloging-in-Publication Data

Names: Fletcher, Patricia.
Title: Why do platypuses lay eggs? And other curious mammal adaptations / Patricia Fletcher.
Description: New York : Gareth Stevens Publishing, 2018. | Series: Odd adaptations | Includes index.
Identifiers: ISBN 9781538204016 (pbk.) | ISBN 9781538204030 (library bound) | ISBN 9781538204023 (6 pack)
Subjects: LCSH: Platypus–Juvenile literature. | Adaptation (Biology)–Juvenile literature.
Classification: LCC QL737.M72 F54 2018 | DDC 599.2'9–dc23

First Edition

Published in 2018 by
Gareth Stevens Publishing
111 East 14th Street, Suite 349
New York, NY 10003

Copyright © 2018 Gareth Stevens Publishing

Designer: Sarah Liddell
Editor: Kristen Nelson

Photo credits: Cover, p. 1 (platypus) Gunter Ziesler/Getty Images; cover, p. 1 (nest) Niccoló Caranti (MUSE)/ Wikimedia Commons; background used throughout Captblack76/Shutterstock.com; pp. 4, 29 (fox and jakal) Eric Isselee/Shutterstock.com; p. 5 SuperStock/Getty Images; p. 6 Butterfly Hunter/Shutterstock.com; p. 7 Ryan M. Bolton/Shutterstock.com; pp. 8–9 cyo bo/Shutterstock.com; p. 9 Eduard Kyslynskyy/Shutterstock.com; p. 10 Oleg Malyshev/Shutterstock.com; p. 11 John E Marriott/Getty Images; p. 12 File Upload Bot (Magnus Manske)/Wikimedia Commons; p. 13 Endless Traveller/Shutterstock.com; p. 14 Dmytro Pylypenko/Shutterstock.com; p. 15 Manuel Lacoste/ Shutterstock.com; p. 16 Tim Zurowski/Shutterstock.com; p. 17 Ingo Arndt/Minden Pictures/Getty Images; p. 18 Flickr upload bot/Wikimedia Commons; p. 19 Nicholas Smythe/Getty Images; p. 21 (arctic hare) critterbiz/Shutterstock.com; p. 21 (snow leopard) Suha Derbent/Shutterstock.com; p. 21 (giraffe) Claudiovidri/Shutterstock.com; p. 21 (cheetah) Jandrie Lombard/Shutterstock.com; p. 21 (wolf) Bildagentur Zoonar GmbH/Shutterstock.com; p. 22 GUIDO BISSATTINI/Shutterstock.com; p. 23 Heush/Wikimedia Commons; p. 24 Calliopejen1/ Wikimedia Commons; p. 25 Fred Bruemmer/Getty Images; p. 26 Isuaneye/Shutterstock.com; p. 27 BP.BomB/ Shutterstock.com; p. 28 Bolid74/Wikimedia Commons; p. 29 (wolf) mariait/Shutterstock.com; p. 29 (dog) photovova/ Shutterstock.com; p. 29 (coyote) outdoorsman/Shutterstock.com.

Printed in China

CONTENTS

Words in the glossary appear in **bold** type the first time they are used in the text.

EGG-LAYING MAMMALS

For a long time, egg-laying mammals called monotremes, such as the platypus, were the most populous kinds of Australian mammals. When marsupials arrived between 71 million and 54 million years ago, they took over many **habitats**. Other kinds of mammals died out. The platypus may have survived by heading to the water!

THE ANCESTORS OF MODERN PLATYPUSES WERE ABLE TO SPEND PART OF THEIR TIME IN THE WATER BECAUSE THEY LAID EGGS. Marsupials, and most other mammals, give birth to live young that would drown in the water. That's why platypuses still lay eggs today. This adaptation helped them survive when the conditions around them changed!

THERE ARE ONLY FIVE SPECIES, OR KINDS, OF MONOTREMES ALIVE TODAY: THE DUCK-BILLED PLATYPUS AND FOUR KINDS OF ECHIDNAS.

ECHIDNA

PLATYPUS

ARE MONOTREMES MAMMALS?

Yes! Like other mammals, monotremes are warm-blooded, which means their body maintains a steady temperature no matter what the surrounding conditions are. They have body hair and a backbone and feed their babies milk from the mother's body. Monotremes don't give birth to live young like other mammals do. That's the only difference—and it's a weird one!

ADAPTATION EDUCATION

Adaptations are changes in the body or behaviors of animals that help them better survive in their habitat. Physical, or body, adaptations include changes in coloring, shape, size, or features. Behavioral adaptations include any changes to the way an animal acts, such as being most active at night. **OFTEN, IT'S EASIER FOR SCIENTISTS TO IDENTIFY WHAT AN ADAPTATION IS FOR THAN WHY IT DEVELOPED IN THE FIRST PLACE!** They study animals in zoos, in their native habitats, and the fossils of animal ancestors to try to learn more. However, there are many odd mammal adaptations we still don't know much about!

FLYING MAMMALS?

The Sunda flying lemur is misnamed—it's not a lemur, and it can't actually fly. It has a **unique** adaptation that allows it to glide on the air from tree to tree in the treetops of the rainforest where it lives. **THE SUNDA FLYING LEMUR HAS A THIN SKIN THAT CONNECTS ITS FACE, LEGS, AND TAIL, HELPING IT "FLY"!**

THE SUNDA FLYING LEMUR IS
A MAMMAL CALLED A COLUGO.
ITS BONES ARE VERY LIGHT AND
THIN, ANOTHER ADAPTATION
THAT MAKES IT WELL SUITED TO
MOVE THE WAY IT DOES!

7

SUCH GREAT HEIGHTS

Giraffes are hard to miss. In fact, they're the tallest land animals on Earth, often growing to be 18 feet (5.5 m) tall! Some scientists think giraffes' long neck is an adaptation that developed so giraffes can reach leaves high in the trees, food other animals couldn't get to.

Giraffes aren't alone in adapting in order to compete less for food. The gerenuk (GEHR-uh-nuhk) is one of many antelope species that live on the African savanna, or grasslands. **TO REACH FOOD OTHER ANTELOPES CAN'T, GERENUKS STAND ON THEIR HIND LEGS!** They've **evolved** to have a long neck and long, thin legs, perfect for how they feed.

NECKING

Giraffes' necks may be really long for a reason other than eating. **WHEN COMPETING FOR A FEMALE GIRAFFE, MALE GIRAFFES WHIP THEIR NECKS BACK AND FORTH, USING THEIR HARD HEAD TO HIT ONE ANOTHER.** Scientists have found that the bigger giraffe commonly wins when giraffes are "necking."

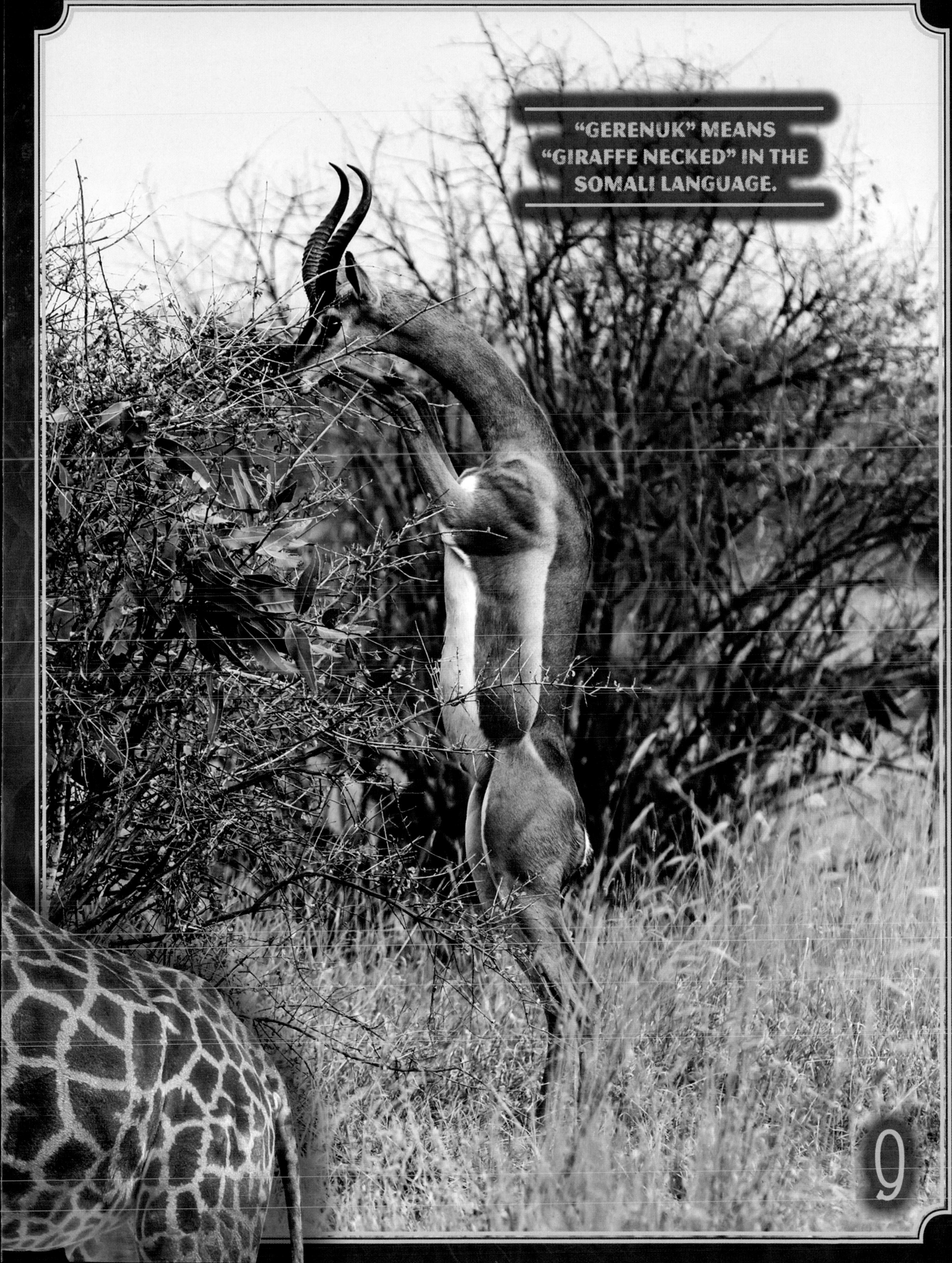

"GERENUK" MEANS "GIRAFFE NECKED" IN THE SOMALI LANGUAGE.

SNACKING BEYOND PLANTS

A mammal's mouth, stomach, and teeth are adapted to what it eats. For example, you might know that cows are herbivores, or animals that eat plants. They have flat teeth perfect for chewing the grasses they like to eat most—except that they don't always eat plants!

COWS AND OTHER HERBIVORES SOMETIMES EAT BIRDS AND OTHER ANIMALS! Scientists think this adaptation could be a behavior used when cows, deer, sheep, and other herbivores don't get the **nutrients** they need from their plant diet. Other scientists think these animals may eat birds simply because they realize they can!

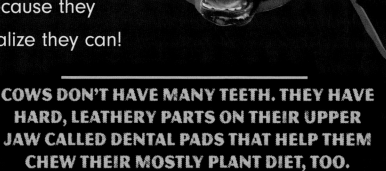

COWS DON'T HAVE MANY TEETH. THEY HAVE HARD, LEATHERY PARTS ON THEIR UPPER JAW CALLED DENTAL PADS THAT HELP THEM CHEW THEIR MOSTLY PLANT DIET, TOO.

DEAD MEAT

Coyotes aren't picky eaters. First of all, they're omnivores, or animals that eat meat and plants. **COYOTES DON'T MIND EATING *DEAD* MEAT EITHER!** Dead animal meat, or carrion, is food for other mammals, too, such as opossums, foxes, and rats.

11

A HUMP OF FAT

Imagine you need to be in the desert for 2 weeks. You would definitely need to bring food and water to survive. Camels live in the desert all the time. **THEY HAVE AN ADAPTATION THAT MEANS THEY DON'T NEED TO LOOK FOR FOOD VERY OFTEN. IT'S THEIR HUMP!** A camel's hump is made of fat the camel has stored so it doesn't have to eat regularly in the desert where food can be hard to find. Camels can have as much as 80 pounds (36 kg) of fat in their hump!

Karakul sheep, which live in a very dry climate as well, also have a body part to store fat in—their tail!

KARAKUL SHEEP

MANY MAMMALS DEVELOP ADAPTATIONS IN ORDER TO BETTER SURVIVE IN THE HOT, DRY CLIMATE OF DESERTS.

NATURAL SUNSCREEN

Hippos can get sunburned easily. They have a great adaptation for the strong sun in their hot African habitats. Hippos **secrete** a liquid that protects them from the sun, keeps their skin moist, and even acts as an antibiotic. What's odd is the color. **IN THE LIGHT, HIPPOS' NATURAL SUNSCREEN LOOKS LIKE BLOOD!**

13

IN THE COLD

Cold weather requires mammals to adapt, too! MUSK OXEN ARE HAIRY MAMMALS—AND THEY GET EVEN HAIRIER DURING THE FREEZING WINTERS OF THEIR ARCTIC HABITAT! Year-round, musk oxen have long outer hairs called guard hairs. When the weather starts to get even colder, they grow an undercoat that helps keep them warm. It falls out when temperatures start to rise.

Hair and fur help water mammals stay warm, too. SEA OTTERS HAVE 130,000 HAIRS PER SQUARE CENTIMETER (0.15 SQ IN) OF SKIN! An otter's fur is so thick, it traps a layer of air near the skin, which keeps the cold water out.

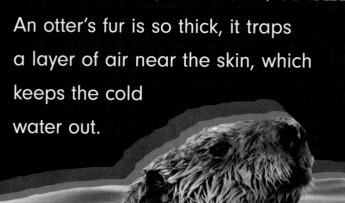

SEA OTTER

BLOWING THE COAT

When it gets colder, many mammals grow more hair. They lose some of it when it gets warmer. You might notice your dog leaves hair just about everywhere when summer starts! When mammals lose hair because the season changes, it's called shedding. It's one adaptation many mammals have!

MUSK OXEN HAVE BEEN
LIVING IN THE ARCTIC FOR
THOUSANDS OF YEARS!

15

If you could sleep through the coldest part of the year, would you? Some mammals do something like that! It's called hibernation. True hibernation is when animals are inactive for a long time. Their breathing and heart rate slow, and their body temperature drops.

SOME KINDS OF GROUND SQUIRRELS MAY HIBERNATE FOR AS LONG AS 9 MONTHS! No one tells them it's time to get settled in underground tunnels they've built. Instead, ground squirrels' blood changes to let them know when to hibernate. Ground squirrels "wake up" every few weeks to move around and go to the bathroom. Then, it's right back to hibernating!

NO BATHROOM BREAKS

UNLIKE GROUND SQUIRRELS, THE BLACK BEAR DOESN'T HAVE TO COME OUT OF HIBERNATION TO PEE! They don't need food or water during their 5 to 7 months of hibernation. While hibernating, the bears' body activity slows down a lot. They only breathe about once every 45 seconds!

GROUND SQUIRREL

16

SCIENTISTS HAVE FOUND THAT
HIBERNATION IS AN ADAPTATION
THAT DEVELOPED AS A WAY
TO DEAL WITH TIMES WHEN
LITTLE FOOD WAS AVAILABLE.

ODD AND VENOMOUS

Poisonous mammals are fairly rare, making their adaptation all the more bizarre and interesting! One kind is a mammal already seen as odd for the female's strange egg-laying behavior: the platypus. Male platypuses have a spike on their back feet that's so poisonous, it can kill small animals that attack!

Could a cute, fuzzy shrew really hurt another animal? Yes! **THE NORTH AMERICAN SHREW SHORT-TAILED SHREW USES ITS POISONOUS BITE TO PARALYZE PREY.** They make the poison, called venom, in body parts called glands near their mouths, and it flows down a **groove** in their teeth into the prey.

A BITE FROM A SHREW PARALYZES AN EARTHWORM OR SMALL MOUSE, BUT IT ONLY CAUSES A PERSON A LITTLE PAIN FOR A FEW DAYS.

NORTH AMERICAN SHORT-TAILED SHREW

POISONOUS PAST

SOME SCIENTISTS BELIEVE THAT MORE MAMMALS WERE VENOMOUS MILLIONS OF YEARS AGO. However, other protective adaptations such as sharp claws and teeth made poisonous bites unnecessary. Venom also works much slower against prey and attackers! In fact, the poisonous mammal the solenodon is being forced from its habitat by dogs and cats!

SOLENODON

COLOR CODE

Mammals are colored how they are for a reason! One coloring adaptation is called camouflage, or an animal's ability to blend in with its surroundings. Some mammals, such as the Arctic hare, use their coloring to hide from predators. **IN THE SUMMER, ARCTIC HARES ARE A BROWNISH GRAY COLOR TO BLEND IN WITH THE ROCKS OF THEIR HABITAT. IN WINTER, THEIR COAT GROWS IN WHITE TO BLEND IN WITH THE SNOW!**

The snow leopard, on the other hand, is hiding from prey! It has a thick white, light gray, or yellowish coat with rings of black or brown. It's well hidden in the rocky, snowy mountains of central Asia!

USING THE PATTERN

Giraffes are one of the most unique zoo animals. **DID YOU KNOW THE RETICULATED PATTERN ON GIRAFFES IS ACTUALLY CAMOUFLAGE?** The patterns or odd markings on some mammals' fur developed to **mimic** the patterns of light and darkness in their habitat. That means giraffes might be easy to spot at the zoo—but tough to spot among the trees of their native habitat!

MAMMALS BLENDING IN

SNOW LEOPARD

ARCTIC HARE

GIRAFFE

CHEETAH

WOLF

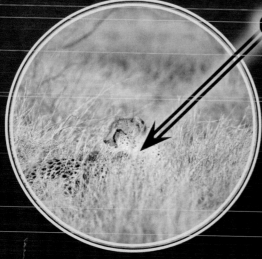

CAMOUFLAGE IS AN
IMPORTANT ADAPTATION
FOR ALL KINDS OF ANIMALS,
NOT JUST MAMMALS.

21

ATTRACTION ADAPTATION

In North America, male deer are known to grow huge antlers. These antlers need to be tough and stiff so they don't break when males use them to fight for a mate. **DEER ANTLERS ARE STRONGER THAN BONE!**

While deer antlers are a familiar sight to many people, a deer with long, sharp teeth, or fangs, isn't. **THE TUFTED DEER HAS BOTH ANTLERS *AND* FANGS!** These adaptations are used to fight for mates. First, male deer attack each other with their short antlers. When one deer is down, the other goes after him with its fangs. That's a lot of work to win a mate!

A BIG RACK

Deer antlers grow as part of the skull. Following mating season, male deer lose their antlers. However, they grow back the following year even bigger than before! As they grow, antlers have a soft covering called velvet. When deer start shedding their velvet, they're getting ready to mate.

A TUFTED DEER'S FANGS MAY LOOK SCARY, BUT THESE DEER ARE FAIRLY SMALL AND SHY.

One of the weirdest-looking mating adaptations might belong to the hooded seal. **MALES TRY TO ATTRACT A MATE BY BLOWING A BALLOON!** It's not a birthday balloon, but instead a part of their nose they can **inflate**. The "balloon" is bright red or pink and draws females during mating season.

That's not the only balloon on the male hooded seal! The animal gets its name from the "hood" on top of its head, a **bladder** it can inflate to show another seal it may attack. When there's no air in it, the bladder hangs on the seal's forehead and looks like a hood!

MORE MILK, PLEASE

Like other mammals, hooded seal mothers make milk for their pups, or babies, to drink. But hooded seal pups don't take their mother's milk long. **THESE PUPS ARE WEANED AFTER ONLY 3 TO 5 DAYS, THE SHORTEST TIME OF ANY MAMMAL!**

HOODED SEAL PUP

24

HOODED SEALS LIVE ALONE
FOR MOST OF THE YEAR,
BUT COME TOGETHER IN
THE SPRING TO MATE.

HUMANS' PART

Animal adaptations often happen because the conditions around an animal change. People can be part of that process! **IRRAWADDY DOLPHINS HAVE HELPED FISHERMEN CATCH MORE FISH!** There has been fishing on the coasts and in the rivers of Southeast Asia so long, this species of dolphin developed a unique behavior. For years, Irrawaddy dolphins drove schools of fish toward the fishermen's nets. It was a great way for the dolphins to get a meal, too!

However, this helpful behavior has slowed as the Irrawaddy dolphin is in danger of dying out in some places, in part because of the fishermen they helped!

MOST IRRAWADDY DOLPHINS LIVE VERY CLOSE TO PEOPLE, WHICH IS LIKELY WHY THEY HAVE ADAPTED TO HUMAN BEHAVIORS! SOME OF THESE DOLPHINS SPEND THEIR WHOLE LIVES IN THE FRESHWATER OF RIVERS IN SOUTHEAST ASIA. OTHERS LIVE JUST A FEW MILES OFF THE COAST.

SHOCKING CHANGES

For more than 10 years, fishermen in the waters Irrawaddy dolphins live in have been using car batteries to create electric shocks in the water. This kills lots of fish, but also harms the dolphin population. The dolphins that still survive no longer seem to trust any fishermen and have learned to stay away more.

Dogs are called man's best friend, and some people believe they can talk to their pet pup. **THAT'S TRUER THAN YOU THINK! DOGS LIKELY BARK TO TELL US SOMETHING—AND WE CAN UNDERSTAND IT!** Many pet owners can tell the difference between a "play" bark and a bark telling of trouble.

Dogs and animals related to them, such as wolves and coyotes, are called canines. Most canines don't bark much. They whine, howl, and make other noises. About 50,000 years ago, dogs evolved away from other canines. They've now lived with people for more than 10,000 years. They've learned to bark when they want our attention. What a strange adaptation!

MOUSE IN THE HOUSE!

A house mouse would normally die from a special poison called rodenticide. However, the Algerian mouse, which can't be killed by this poison, mated with house mice, making babies that are also resistant to the poison! How did they meet? People traveling between the places where they live brought them together by accident!

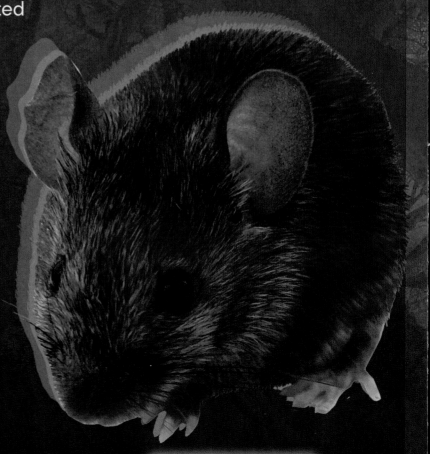

CANIDAE

FOX

WOLF

DOG

COYOTE

JACKAL

DOGS BELONG TO THE ANIMAL FAMILY CANIDAE. DOGS ARE THE ONLY ONES THAT BARK A LOT!

GLOSSARY

ancestor: an animal that lived before others in its family tree

bladder: a body part that expands and fills with gas

develop: to grow and change

evolve: to grow and change over time

groove: a narrow space cut into something

habitat: the natural place where an animal or plant lives

inflate: to fill with gas

mimic: to copy

nutrient: something a living thing needs to grow and stay alive

paralyze: to make unable to move

reticulated: covered with crisscrossing lines, like a net

secrete: to produce and release

unique: one of a kind

wean: to adapt a young animal to no longer drinking milk from its mother

FOR MORE INFORMATION

BOOKS

Beaumont, Holly. *Why Do Monkeys and Other Mammals Have Fur?* Chicago, IL: Heinemann Raintree, 2016.

Kras, Sara Louise. *Platypuses.* Mankato, MN: Capstone Press, 2010.

Schafer, Susan. *Invasive Mammals.* New York, NY: Cavendish Square Publishing, 2016.

WEBSITES

Mammals
kids.nationalgeographic.com/animals/hubs/mammals/
Review what features a mammal has and find links to more information about many kinds of mammals.

Top 10 Animal Adaptations
www.animalplanet.com/wild-animals/animal-adaptations/
Mammals aren't the only animals with adaptations! Find out about more on this website.

INDEX